DANGERS OF PROCRASTINATION

HOW TO GET THINGS DONE AND THE MINDSET BEHIND PROCRASTINATION

Russell R. Bowie

Introduction

The Publisher has attempted to be as accurate and detailed as possible, due to the Internet's propensity to change quickly, the Publisher does not at any time guarantee or represent that the contents of this report are accurate. Despite all reasonable efforts to ensure the accuracy of the information in this publication, the Publisher disclaims all responsibility for any errors, omissions, or other readings of the material.

Any apparent slights towards specific individuals, organizations, or groups are unintentional. Like everything else in life, there are no assurances of financial success for authors of how-to books. Readers are urged to act appropriately and respond based on their judgment of their particular situations.

The purpose of this book is not to provide accounting, financial, legal, or commercial advice. We fervently advise all readers to speak with knowledgeable authorities in the fields of law, business, accounting, and finance. For ease of reading, printing this book is advised.

Russell R. Bowie

Basics of procrastination

Because procrastination has such a wide range, people need to become familiar with its fundamentals before they can fully comprehend and conquer their procrastination environment of behavior. You can obtain a better knowledge of the fundamentals of procrastination by reading the information below.

Procrastination is the act of putting off or completing less important chores in favor of those that are more urgent. This is another tendency when people choose to do enjoyable activities instead of less enjoyable ones, only to discover that they have postponed important tasks, sometimes even until the very last minute. The antithesis of optimal productivity is procrastination. Producing is moving forward and working to complete tasks, whereas procrastinating means delaying tasks until later—likely never. Your life may be filled with humiliation if you engage in this behavior. Due to their lethargy, inability to focus on the crucial duties at hand, and the human habit of being easily lured to more immediate and easy gratifications, there are even situations where some people are blaming themselves. Sometimes delaying something is a good idea since it gives you more time to think things through and plan your course of action.

The benefit of procrastination is that it gives people the time they need to analyze complex problems and come up with ideas. It is unavoidable that people will encounter situations where procrastination is a good habit to adopt. But you must avoid procrastinating if it has the potential to turn into a dangerous habit and have a bad impact on your life. The fundamentals of procrastination are not sufficient. People need to know the specifics to understand things more clearly.

motives for their procrastination. People frequently put things off for the following motives:
Insufficient motivation

Lack of enthusiasm

Lack of proficiency

both success and failure-related phobia

 Stress

Being lazy

Absence of Discipline

lack of expertise

Perfectionism

These are the causes that prompt people to put things off, and if they are not appropriately addressed, they will undoubtedly have bad effects. Other causes include lack of knowledge or understanding of what has to be done, lack of enthusiasm, lack of concern about whether something is done or not, lack of mood or initiative to start things, and many more. There are no justifiable grounds to allow yourself to become ensnared in this habit because of the drawbacks that this practice brings. The good news is that procrastination can be conquered and defeated in various ways.

People only need to make an effort to adopt these behaviors and put them into practice. There are still more effective techniques to overcome procrastination in addition to understanding the basics of the behavior and the causes of procrastination in people. Change your environment to prevent procrastination, make a timeline, find inspiration, divide larger activities into smaller, more doable chores, and the list goes on.

Making a Timeline

Many people today struggle with the procrastination phenomenon. These people frequently have busy schedules and deadlines that are stressful, yet despite the urgency of the work, they procrastinate, cling to the habit of delaying things or carrying out less important chores. One efficient method of breaking this tendency is by making a timetable. The significance of developing a timeline and its advantages are as follows.

Fighting conflicting priorities, failure fear, high stress, and a perfectionist attitude have all been combated through procrastination. Delaying or postponing a task, however, can result in issues and lower-than-expected work quality. Additionally, this practice can cause tension, anxiety, and resentment. It can also result in longer workdays and missed chances. Consider strategies to completely tackle procrastination if it starts to undermine your productivity.People frequently have deadlines, but instead of finishing their work, they check their social media and email accounts, browse blogs and forums, and watch videos. You must be employed, yet you lack the desire and drive to carry out your duties. In situations like these, people waste their free time and put off crucial things they should be completed until it is too late. People start to panic and freak out when they discover it is already late. They start to regret not getting started sooner.

In reality, procrastination is a poor habit that prevents people from achieving better outcomes in life. One of the many effective strategies for overcoming procrastination is to create a timeline. You should think about it if you don't want this habit to control your life. You must make your task or timetable schedule. By doing so, you are giving each task enough time, increasing your chances of meeting all of your deadlines.

You can use a spreadsheet, diary, or to-do list to create your timetable or timeline. Select the device that works flawlessly for you. You are inspired to work more and evaluate your circumstances when deadlines are set. Additionally, you may estimate how long various chores and projects will take you. Make your deadline your boss and try not to put things off since you will regret it in the long run. You also need to remember that you have to complete something at the end of every planned session. Deadlines can be frustrating, particularly if you continue to practice procrastination. This is typically what prevents you from attaining the outcomes you want. Just keep in mind that setting up a timetable and task plan are excellent techniques to combat frustration and procrastination as well. You will be able to fulfill deadlines and lead an enjoyable and successful life if you maintain your work, tasks, and responsibilities and do not procrastinate.

10

Improving Your Environment for Procrastination

Nowadays, many people practice the prevalent habit of procrastinating in their daily lives. They frequently put off or postpone completing important duties in favor of wasting time on unimportant activities. The good news is that eliminating the procrastinating environment is a great strategy to break this behavior. The following suggestions will help you make changes to your procrastinating environment.

your surroundings

You may procrastinate for a variety of reasons, therefore in order to stop this habit from taking over your life, you need to use the correct strategy to change your environment. Your surroundings may directly affect how productive you are. It is vital to assess whether or not your surroundings and workspace excite you in order to avoid becoming complacent. Determine whether the environment you are in encourages positive or negative emotions. Consider practical solutions to improve and alter your surroundings so that it is more suitable and conducive to functioning if your environment tends to evoke unpleasant emotions and moods. There are a number of techniques to achieve this, like clearing the trash and clutter from your desk or table, switching out your lightbulbs for brighter ones, and spritzing therapeutic and scented air until your senses are fully awakened. Here are some additional helpful strategies for improving your environment for procrastination:

1. Improve the aesthetic appeal of your surroundings or place It's important to remember that your workplace doubles as your home, so it should be inviting and energetic. An unpleasant setting will only encourage you to put things off. Therefore, it's important to maintain a beautiful environment so that you can be inspired and motivated to complete your work. It makes perfect sense to add visual impact to your workspace.

2. Add flowers

Adding flowers to your dreary surroundings or workspace is an excellent method to breathe new life into them. Use living or oxygen-producing plants as opposed to artificial ones. These plants will begin to flourish together with you and act as a mirror of who you are. Make time to spend in the outdoors and get connected to the natural world.

3. Make your surroundings smell pleasant

Your productivity will be significantly impacted by a clean and fresh environment. Working in a space that makes you feel good and smell good is strangely engaging and motivated.

4. Stream soothing music.

Some people put things off because their surroundings are chaotic or difficult. If you are truly committed to breaking your procrastination habit, you must alter this atmosphere. Playing soothing music will motivate you to work harder and finish your responsibilities on time. You might try various musical genres to see if it has any impact on your level of productivity or tension. If you don't want to disturb people, you can wear headphones.

5. Make your space your own.

Your performance and productivity are impacted by your workspace. Change your surroundings by making your area more pleasant and functional if you don't want to procrastinate. This is a great approach to improving your mood and getting things done.

Break Things Down Into More Manageable Steps

Some people believe that procrastination is the soul's demise, yet others do not share this opinion. Whatever opinions and insights people may have on the subject, procrastination is still a habit that needs to be changed and thoroughly conquered, it seems.

Inspiration

There are various strategies for breaking this habit. Get motivated and surround yourself with others who will motivate and inspire you if you want to quit putting off tasks. The actions listed below can help you get motivated and effectively stop procrastinating.

1. Spend time with those who will motivate and inspire you to act. It is a given that spending time with deserving and diligent individuals will inspire you to work and take action more than inaction. You must be aware that other individuals could affect how you

behave. You must make sure that the only people that inspire you are those who have a positive impact on your life.

Determine your coworkers and those who inspire you to work hard and improve. Spend more time with those that are driven and hardworking. To get further advice on how to cope with procrastination effectively, you may also spend time with personal development professionals.

2. Find an Encouraging Friend

It is simpler to stop procrastinating behavior when you have the greatest partner. The person you choose for your ideal body must also have more ambitious life ambitions. Even if it's not required for you to share the same objectives, you will both be responsible for each other's plans and aims. It is advantageous to have different objectives so that you can learn from one another. Talk to your friend frequently, making time to discuss each other's goals and the progress being made toward reaching them. This action motivates you to act.

3. Look for others who have successfully broken their procrastination behavior and get motivation from them.

There are times in life when you need to look for others who have been in your shoes and learn how they managed to succeed in getting things done if you want to accomplish things and be successful. Connect with them once you've located them. Seeing evidence that your goals can be reached may inspire you to act and lead a more active life.

If you truly want to live a more positive life, you should surround yourself with positive people. This idea also holds for getting rid of procrastination. Be among people who motivate you to pursue your goals with action, persistence, and hard effort rather than simply being with those who will merely adhere to your procrastination environment.

Use Uplifting Phrases to

Motivate You

It may be necessary to give previous attention to the practice or act of procrastinating, delaying, or putting off things. Even if someone is intelligent, procrastination can cause them to consistently be late and behind schedule on practically every activity or assignment. The following information will show you how to stop procrastinating by breaking tasks down into smaller chunks.

Procrastination is a difficult habit to break. Perhaps the ability of procrastinators to put off even the simplest activities that they think they can complete is a common trait. The worst-case scenario is that those who procrastinate end up anxious and taking their time. You must overcome procrastination if you want to be a successful and high-functioning person. To maintain productivity and get your life back on track, this is necessary.

Breaking things down into smaller parts may help you avoid procrastination and pressure, as it won't be as difficult for you to complete duties on time. Looking at the full scope of your responsibilities may merely depress you and cause you to put them off. The best way to stop procrastinating is not to break things down into smaller pieces. Other options include the following:

1. Establishing a timeline or calendar. List all of the tasks that must be completed along with their corresponding due dates.

2. Setting project priorities: Arrange projects and tasks according to their priority. Remember to keep deadlines and priorities in mind.

3. Setting aside more time—allot more time to do tasks and meet deadlines. Putting everything off till the last minute can only lead to disaster and stress.

4. Creating a detailed goal-setting and action plan is a great technique to overcome procrastination.

5. Create a welcoming and appealing work atmosphere – To stop procrastinating, you need to create a calm and pleasant setting. Working with numerous files can only reduce productivity.

The Value of Dividing Tasks into Smaller Steps Breaking projects into digestible portions will help you complete tasks and meet your objectives efficiently and practically. Spend time finishing difficult jobs. Making the process manageable requires breaking it up into smaller steps. People may put off doing their tasks because they find it to be too overwhelming. You can concentrate on one step or part at a time if you break these tasks down into smaller pieces. Try to further split things down if you find yourself putting off tasks. Your mission will become clear to you soon, and you'll have the drive and enthusiasm to get things done right away. The ideal course of action is to focus on the current phase or stage and complete it to the best of your ability without considering or worrying about the subsequent one. You can now move on to the following step or immediate component. Focusing on the quantity and difficulty of the duties will only make you feel overwhelmed and encourage delay. No matter how difficult a project may be, it can be broken down into smaller jobs or phases. Simply disregard the larger picture at first and focus on completing each assignment in turn.

Russell R. Bowie

Consider Your Goals and Tell Others About Them

Because words have such power, they can influence, inspire, and motivate listeners. However, these can also discourage, dismiss, and dissuade. Therefore, it is imperative that you constantly consider motivating terms. With the power of your words, you can sow the seeds of your success. Along the way, you have the opportunity to show the world who, what, and how you really are.

Be Positive

The appropriate words should always be chosen and delivered, no matter what the aim. When you have a lot of obligations and tasks to complete, you may feel as though you should put things off until tomorrow. Procrastination is a behavior that prevents people from being more productive and goal-oriented. There are many methods to achieve this and get things done, and one effective method of doing this is by thinking about encouraging words to get you inspired. Consider encouraging remarks that motivate you to keep going. This cannot be captured in a single photo. You must complete each of your responsibilities individually. Before you can fully accomplish something, you really need to take a lot of little steps. Never let those statements ruin your day since they will only cause you to become sidetracked. Your level of concentration and productivity will suffer in such a situation. Consider phrases that will serve as a reminder to get the things done today so that tomorrow can be a nice day for other routines and tasks.

Keep in mind that thinking positive thoughts lead to positive thinking and great outcomes. Change your environment and choose to be in a place where others offer their uplifting or wise words if the words you are hearing in your current setting have a negative impact on you or cause you to put off tasks. Thinking about these ideas will motivate you to break negative behaviors, improve yourself, and accomplish your objectives. Positive words can genuinely alter your thoughts, which can affect both your mood and your decision-making. As long as you have the genuine determination and are willing to put out the necessary effort, these can also feed your enthusiasm and give you the impression that you can do anything. If you also want to stop procrastinating, you can find motivation by thinking of encouraging words. This makes it easier for you to get things done without procrastinating, hurrying, or worrying at the last minute.

Work on Achieving Your

Goals

You can run across a lot of questions and confusions while you figure out what it is that you really want to do. Some claim that you must distinguish between your wants and necessities in order to consider and decide what you want. Self-discovery is necessary to determine what you genuinely want. Finding out what you actually want to do will help you stop procrastinating if that is a habit you have. The following advice will help you identify your true priorities and show you how they may prevent procrastination.

Describe it

It is inevitable that people will encounter a variety of situations in life that will confound them and make it challenging for them to choose what they must do and what they truly desire in life. These are the kinds of situations that demotivate people and cause them to put things off. You must deal with and try to overcome these issues if you find that you are beginning to put off tasks. You must have the right attitude and perspective. Consider your goals carefully and consider how you might best communicate them to others. You could think about taking the following actions:

1. Figure Out What You Are Really Passionate About If a new task or object doesn't pique your interest or inspire you, you'll need to come up with creative ways to make it so you'll be inspired to do it.

2. Request input from friends and family

The majority of the time, those closest to you are aware of your goals, dreams, and other significant objectives. Therefore, since your closest friends and family members are the ones who know you best, they can offer criticism if you're having trouble figuring out what you actually want to accomplish.

Talk to the people you can really trust, and ask them to give you an honest appraisal of where they see your future in life. You should nonetheless be ready because you could not agree with all of the responses that are provided to you. Additionally, you can get feedback on your strengths and flaws from friends and family members.

3. Engage in some visualization or introspection

If you want to discover what it is that you truly want to achieve in life, you can conduct some introspection. You can pick which area or stage of your life you wished to pursue by reflecting on both the happy and the sad ones. You become more driven and focused to finish your assignment if you are clear about what it is that you need to concentrate on. In a sense, you are also breaking the procrastinating habit in this way. It is true that people who lack life direction or a deadline for tasks to be done tend to postpone more frequently. There are many effective ways to think about and choose what you really want to achieve in life, but the most crucial thing is that you must concentrate on what you want and not on the things that you do not want. You should also be able to share what you want with others to inspire them and aid them in determining what they too need to achieve.

Give Yourself a Break

Procrastination generally refers to a fundamental issue in human nature that has to do with time. This behavior is defined by the propensity to put off tasks and the notion that it is pointless to complete them today if they may be completed tomorrow. The majority of procrastinators focused on this idea, and the number of people with this mindset is now rising. The power to break this habit is in your hands, so do it. There are several accounts of how many people have succeeded in kicking the habit, and they reward themselves by doing so.

Reach Your Objectives and Reward Yourself

Every time you complete a task or meet your objective, you should treat yourself to show your appreciation for the effort. Many people are so busy working constantly that they neglect to unwind and treat themselves. A quick break might help you feel more invigorated and productive. If you work lengthy hours, you risk being fatigued and worn out, which can lead to procrastination. You must go ahead and reward yourself whenever you complete tasks and reach little milestones. It's not strictly necessary for you to select the most expensive prize. As long as these things make you happy, even simple ones will do. You could treat yourself to these things:

1. Take in a film at night
Once everything is finished, you can watch a movie with your friends or family. Although it may not seem like much, many people value this modest gesture.

2. Take a relaxing bath.

You can treat yourself to a lengthy, relaxing bubble bath at the end of the day as a reward for all of your hard work and effort.

3. Purchase and read your favorite book.
You frequently put aside several of your interests, including reading, because of your busy job and business schedules. When you've successfully overcome procrastination and completed your tasks, you may now treat yourself to your favorite book and enjoy reading.

4. Visiting a salon
Luxurious beauty treatment at your preferred salon is another way to treat yourself for a job well done. When you achieve your goals and complete tasks, you deserve to treat yourself to a vacation to a beauty salon where you may relax and refresh. You can feel and look better with a facial, manicure, or pedicure, and these small but meaningful adjustments might be your greatest motivators.

5. Arrange a Trip
One of the most typical ways to treat yourself is to travel or leave town. You could treat yourself to a luxurious vacation if your schedule and finances would permit it. A reward or indulgence that is promised after a busy day is a fantastic motivator. You have a lot of options when it comes to rewarding yourself. You can have a nice massage, buy new clothes, indulge in your favorite music, and more. You should only do things and things that will benefit you, not things or things that will

have negative effects or implications. You truly deserve a reward because you put up the necessary effort to complete the tasks at hand.

Russell R. Bowie

Rewards of Prompt Action

You can make things happen. To reach your goals, you just need to get rid of negative attitudes like poor time management and procrastination from your system and replace them with good ones. Never feel overwhelmed or discouraged when you are going to do larger chores. To better focus on each work, break up these larger chores into smaller, more manageable ones. You'll finally realize that you've accomplished everything that needed to be done. You can only gain from getting things done if you stop putting off completing them and start doing them right now. The advantages of completing tasks on time and according to the plan include the following.

1. Finishing tasks makes you feel relaxed.
There are several advantages to getting things done for both your business and personal lives. A fantastic way to simultaneously feel in charge and at ease is to gather your belongings, organize and organize them, and then transform them into valuable items and useful information.

2. You have more discretion as a result.
You are allowed freedom of choice once you have previously accomplished something. The results of your work, commitments, and activities that are monitored

by your getting things done system can be used to inform your decision. You can also utilize your intuition to establish your priorities.

3. Completing tasks enables you to make and honor commitments.
When you complete tasks, you will enjoy not forgetting or putting things off since you will have reached the point where you are ultimately content with the results of your labor. You gain the ability and correct attitude to recall and uphold commitments as you complete tasks.

4. This encourages creative thinking.
Rethinking ideas and activities from scratch is a great method to use advanced thinking. You will undoubtedly reach your objective if you focus on the tasks at hand. Getting things done gives you time to plan out your next activity or endeavor.

5. Completing tasks helps you pursue your dreams.
You can achieve your dreams in a structured way by accomplishing things. You can bargain with yourself and decide what you need to do for your future when you are working on things and finishing them.

6. You become more effective and productive when you complete tasks.
You become more organized and persistent with your job or chores when you overcome procrastination. This has the added benefit of increasing your productivity and effectiveness. When you adopt a good attitude and

complete tasks to the best of your ability, you can achieve enormous benefits. Getting things done may also be a great foundation for you to grow as a person. Getting things done fosters strong individual productivity.

www.ingramcontent.com/pod-product-compliance
Lightning Source LLC
Chambersburg PA
CBHW060231170726
48004CB00004BA/1512